MW00368576

Many People, Many Cultures

Harcourt
SCHOOL PUBLISHERS

Visit *The Learning Site!* www.harcourtschool.com

World Cultures

Our world is made up of many cultures. **Culture** is a group's way of life. Food and clothes are part of it. Art and music are, too. A **language** is also a part of culture. Language is the words people speak and write.

A market in Ghana

A family in Spain

In Ghana, people sell and buy fruit at the market. Children listen to stories about a spider.

In Spain, family members eat lunch together. The people like to dance.

Reading Check (Focus Skill) **Recall and Retell**

What is culture?

Learning About Cultures

People show their cultures in different ways. Some people use music or dance. Others wear special clothes.

Mask from Colombia

Mud cloth from Mali

Kimono from Japan

Hat from Peru

Maracas from Mexico

❶ What do these things show about culture?

❷ How can you use these things to compare cultures?

Many People, One Country

Some people come to a new country. They are called **immigrants**. They want a better life. They find new jobs. They learn new ways to do things.

Immigrants at Ellis Island long ago.

Games are part of our culture.

Immigrants learn a new culture. They bring their own cultures, too. They bring different ideas. We can all share ideas. We can learn new things.

Reading Check Focus Skill **Recall and Retell** Why do people come to new countries?

Amy Tan

Amy Tan was born in the United States. Her parents were born in China. Amy liked to write when she was young. She wrote about her library. Her story won a prize!

Time

1952

Born

1969 •————
Finishes high school
in Switzerland

1985 •————
Takes a writing class that
leads to her first book

Now Amy Tan writes stories about her family. She tells about the past. She tells about her Chinese culture.

Amy Tan is proud of her family. She is proud of her culture.

Present

1989
Publishes her first book,
The Joy Luck Club

Celebrating Culture

Families have **traditions**. These are special ways to do things. Traditions are passed from older people to children. Different families may do different things. But they are the same in many ways.

A family celebration

Luz's family celebrates Easter.

David's family is Jewish. Every Friday, the family has a special meal.

Luz's family is Mexican American. On holidays they visit Luz's grandmother.

Reading Check **Compare and Contrast** How are families different?

Recognizing Americans

Many Americans do important work. **Scientists** use tools to look at things. They learn about the world.

Thomas Edison made the first light bulb. George Washington Carver helped farmers.

Thomas Edison

George Washington Carver

Artists do important work, too. Ieoh Ming Pei is an artist. He designs large buildings.

Gloria Estefan writes songs. She sings and dances. She shares her culture.

Reading Check (Focus Skill) **Recall and Retell** Who are some important Americans?

Ieoh Ming Pei

Gloria Estefan

Activity 1

Match each word to its meaning.

immigrant   language   culture

tradition   scientist

1. a special way to do things that is passed from older people to children

2. a group's way of life

3. someone who comes to live in a new country

4. a person who uses tools to learn about the world

5. words that people speak and write

Activity 2

Look at the list of words. Put the words in a chart like this one. Then use a dictionary. Learn what the words mean.

culture   custom   diversity

tradition   immigrant   invention

language   scientist

		I Know	Sounds Familiar	Don't Know
	culture			✓
○	language		✓	
	tradition	✓		

Recall and Retell Who are immigrants?

1. **Vocabulary** What is **culture**?

2. Why are there many cultures in the United States?

3. What are some family traditions?

4. Why is it good for our country to have many cultures?

Activity

Draw a Picture There are many traditions. Think of a tradition you know. Then draw a picture of it. Write a sentence about it.